Embracing
the Buddha Within

THE FOUR NOBLE TRUTHS
A JOURNEY TO ENLIGHTENMENT

CIDER MILL PRESS

BOOK PUBLISHERS

Kennebunkport, Maine

The text for this book comes from the translation
of *The Gospel of Buddha Compiled from Ancient Records* by Paul Carus, Copyright 1915.
The bulk of its contents are from the ancient Buddhist canon.
Edited by Carlo De Vito and Diana Ceres

This book may be ordered by mail from the publisher. Please include $3.99 for postage and handling.
Please support your local bookseller first!

Books published by Cider Mill Press Book Publishers are available at special discounts for bulk purchases in the United States
by corporations, institutions, and other organizations. For more information, please contact the publisher.

Cider Mill Press Book Publishers
"Where good books are ready for press"
12 Spring Street
PO Box 454
Kennebunkport, Maine 04046

Visit us on the web!
www.cidermillpress.com

Design by Alicia Freile and Haylea Bridle, Tango Media
Typeset by Candice Fitzgibbons
Typography: Handle Old Style, Josefin Sans, MrsEaves, and Odette
Printed in China

1 2 3 4 5 6 7 8 9 0
First Edition

Table of Contents

Introduction

Gautama Buddha was a sage and is known as the founder of Buddhism. Early historians placed his lifetime as circa 563 BCE to 483 BCE. A native of the ancient Himalayan foothills, Gautama taught primarily in northeastern India.

According to the early Buddhist texts, after realizing meditative *jhana* was the path to enlightenment, but that extreme self-denial didn't work, Gautama discovered what is known as the Middle Way. This path is one of moderation from the extremes of self-indulgence and self-mortification.

Following a particular incident of realization, Gautama was seated under a Bodhi tree. He vowed to stay under this tree until he reached the supreme truth. At the age of 35, after 49 consecutive days of meditation, Gautama attained full enlightenment. From that time on, he was known to his followers as the Buddha or "The Enlightened One."

At the time of his awakening, Gautama discovered the cause of all suffering and the steps to eliminate it. These discoveries, also known as the Four Noble Truths, are at the heart of all Buddhist teachings. When these truths are mastered, anyone can attain a state of supreme liberation or Nirvana.

For the rest of his life, the Buddha traveled to many regions to share his teachings with others. From the outset, Buddhism was open to all races and classes. These principals and ideals remain intact to this day.

About this Book

This book contains 108 quotations from the ancient Buddhist texts. You may treat each quote like a bead on the Buddhist mala, meditating upon each one, as you work your way to its end. Or you can open this book up to any page and allow that quotation to serve as your daily inspiration or meditation.

Because the Buddha's teachings center on the Four Noble Truths, this book is divided into four sections, one for each Noble Truth.

The first Noble Truth states that we all suffer. It was this first truth that incited the Buddha to begin his quest for enlightenment. The quotes in this first section relate to this initial truth.

The second Noble Truth states that the mind is the source of all suffering. The Buddha taught that by wanting or not wanting something, we create a cycle of suffering. The quotes in this second section are specific to this truth.

The third Noble Truth states that suffering can end. By working to control our mind, we can begin to end our suffering. The quotes in this third section serve to inspire us to move in this direction.

The fourth Noble Truth, also known as the Eightfold Path, shows how we can transcend all suffering by following the path of rightful living. It takes practice to transcend suffering. For many it is a lifetime's work or that of many lifetimes. The quotes in this final section center on this important path for all seekers of enlightenment and true peace.

As the Buddha stated to his first disciples, "He who recognizes the existence of suffering, its cause, its remedy, and its cessation has fathomed the four noble truths. He will walk in the right path. Right views will be the torch to light his way. Right aspirations will be his guide. Right speech will be his dwelling-place on the road. His gait will be straight, for it is right behavior. His refreshments will be the right way of earning his livelihood. Right efforts will be his steps; right thoughts his breath; and right contemplation will give him the peace that follows in his footprints."

The Four Noble Truths

Suffering exists.

Suffering has an origin.

Suffering can end.

The Eightfold Path of rightful living is the way out suffering.

The Eightfold Path

Right View

Right Intention

Right Speech

Right Action

Right Livelihood

Right Effort

Right Mindfulness

Right Concentration

Suffering exists.

THE CAUSE OF ALL SORROW
LIES AT THE VERY BEGINNING;
IT IS HIDDEN IN THE
IGNORANCE FROM WHICH
LIFE GROWS.

The Buddha...

was grieved at the ills of life.

He saw the vanity in worldly happiness
and sought salvation in the one thing
that will not fade or perish,
but will abide forever and ever.

Everything is *transient*
and **nothing endures.**

There is birth and death,
growth and decay; there is
combination and separation.

THE GLORY OF THE WORLD IS
LIKE A FLOWER:
IT STANDS IN FULL BLOOM
IN THE MORNING
AND FADES
IN THE HEAT OF THE DAY.

Is there nothing **permanent** in the world?

Is there in the universal turmoil no resting-place
where our troubled heart can **find peace?**

Is there nothing **everlasting?**

Oh, that we could have
cessation of anxiety,
that our burning desires would be extinguished!

When shall the mind become
tranquil and composed?

You will not be punished for your anger, you will be punished by your anger.

Holding on to anger is like
grasping a hot coal with the intent
of throwing it at someone else;
you are the one who gets burned.

The *tongue* like a sharp knife...
kills without drawing blood.

LIKE EVERYTHING
ELSE IN NATURE,
THE LIFE OF MAN
IS SUBJECT TO THE LAW
OF CAUSE AND EFFECT.

Without health
life is not life;
it is only a state of
languor and suffering
an image of death.

All things appear and disappear
because of the concurrence of
causes and conditions.

Nothing ever exists entirely alone;
everything is in relation to **everything else.**

VIRTUE IS PERSECUTED MORE
BY **THE WICKED** THAN IT IS
LOVED BY **THE GOOD.**

All is Samsara.

Wherever his karma continues,
there will be suffering and woe.

Ye that long for life,

know that **immortality**

is hidden in transiency.

The things of the world and its
inhabitants are subject to change.

They are combinations of elements that
existed before, and all living creatures
are what their past actions made them;
for the law of cause and effect is
uniform and without exception.

There is misery in the world of Samsara; there is much misery and pain.

But greater than all the misery is the bliss of truth.

What joy or pleasure can men take...
when they know they must
soon wither and pine away!

This man is sick...

We are all subject to such conditions:
  the poor and the rich, the ignorant and
  the wise, all creatures that have bodies,
  are liable to the same calamity.

ALL OVER THE WORLD
IT IS THE SAME.

HE WHO BEGINS LIFE
MUST END IT.

THERE IS NO ESCAPE
FROM DEATH.

I see everywhere the impression of change;
therefore, my heart is heavy.

Men grow old, sicken, and die.

That is enough to take away the zest of life.

All combination is subject to **separation**, and we cannot escape birth, disease, old age, and death.

Everything…is burning.

The eye is burning, all the senses are burning,
thoughts are burning.

They are burning with the fire of lust.

There is anger, there is ignorance, there is hatred,
and as long as the fire finds inflammable things
upon which it can feed, so long will it burn,
and there will be birth and death, decay, grief,
lamentation, suffering, despair, and sorrow.

The profit I derived from adoring the fire was continuance in the wheel of **individuality** with all its sorrows and vanities.

Birth is attended with pain, decay is painful,
disease is painful, death is painful.

Union with the unpleasant is painful,
painful is separation from the pleasant;
and any craving that is unsatisfied,
that too is painful.

In brief, bodily conditions which
spring from attachment are painful.

Suffering has an origin.

WHEREVER YOU LOOK,
THERE IS A RUSHING AND A STRUGGLING, AND AN EAGER PURSUIT OF PLEASURE.

THERE IS A PANIC FLIGHT FROM PAIN AND DEATH, AND HOT ARE THE FLAMES OF BURNING DESIRES.

In the sky, there is no distinction of east and west;

people create distinctions out of their own minds and then believe them to be true.

Surrender the grasping disposition
of selfishness, and you will attain to
that calm state of mind which conveys
**perfect peace, goodness,
and wisdom.**

YOU ONLY LOSE
WHAT YOU CLING TO.

It is a **man's own mind,**

not his enemy or foe,

that lures him to evil ways.

There is nothing more dreadful
than the habit of doubt.

Doubt separates people. It is a poison
that disintegrates friendships and
breaks up pleasant relations.

It is a thorn that irritates and hurts;
it is a sword that kills.

In a controversy the instant we
feel anger we have already ceased
striving for the truth, and have begun
striving for ourselves.

Ambition is like love,

impatient both of

delays and rivals.

SELF BEGETS SELFISHNESS.

Do not overrate what you
have received, nor envy others.

He who envies others does not
obtain peace of mind.

That of your heart which cannot or
will not develop into Buddha must perish,
for it is mere illusion and unreal;
it is the source of your error;
it is the cause of your misery.

Indulge in lust but a little,
and lust like a child will grow.

Wield worldly power and you
will be **burdened with cares.**

I pray thee, pity me not.

Rather pity those who are burdened
with the cares of royalty
and the worry of great riches.

They enjoy them in fear and trembling,
for they are constantly threatened
with a loss of those boons
on whose possession their hearts are set,
and when they die they cannot take along
either their gold or the kingly diadem.

SURELY IF LIVING CREATURES
SAW THE RESULTS OF ALL THEIR
EVIL DEEDS, THEY WOULD TURN
AWAY FROM THEM IN DISGUST.

BUT SELFHOOD BLINDS THEM,
AND THEY CLING TO THEIR
OBNOXIOUS DESIRES.

They crave pleasure for themselves
and they cause pain to others;
when death destroys their individuality,
they find no peace; their thirst for existence abides
and their selfhood reappears in new births.

Thus they continue to move in the coil and can find **no escape** from the hell of their own making.

And how **empty** are their pleasures,
how **vain** are their endeavors!

Hollow like the plantain-tree and
without contents like the bubble.

Men go astray because they think that delusion is better than truth.

Rather than truth they follow error, which is pleasant to look at in the beginning but in the end causes anxiety, tribulation, and misery.

The renewed births of selfhood
are the cause of suffering,
old age, sickness, and death.

They produce lamentation,
anxiety, and despair.

THE CLEAVING TO THINGS,
COVETOUSNESS, AND
SENSUALITY INHERITED
FROM FORMER EXISTENCES,
ARE THE CAUSES OF THE MISERY
AND VANITY IN THE WORLD.

The existence of self is an illusion,
and there is no wrong in this world,
no vice, no evil, except what flows
from the assertion of self.

There is **self** and there is **truth**.

Where self is, **truth is not**.

Where truth is, **self is not**.

BLISS CANNOT BE SOLD.

Self is the yearning for pleasure
and the lust after vanity.

Truth is the correct
comprehension of things;
it is the permanent and everlasting,
the real in all existence,
the bliss of righteousness.

The truth remains
hidden from him
who is in the bondage
of hate and desire.

HE WHO FILLS HIS LAMP
WITH WATER WILL NOT
DISPEL THE DARKNESS,
AND HE WHO TRIES TO
LIGHT A FIRE WITH
ROTTEN WOOD WILL FAIL.

How can anyone be free
from self by leading a wretched life,

if he does not succeed in quenching
the fires of lust, if he still hankers after
either worldly or heavenly pleasures.

Verily, it is that craving which causes
the renewal of existence, accompanied
by sensual delight, seeking satisfaction
now here, now there, the craving
for the gratification of the passions,
the craving for a future life, and the
craving for happiness in this life.

Suffering Can End

Truth knows neither birth nor death; it has

no beginning and no end.

Welcome the truth.

The truth is the immortal part of mind.

BODIES FALL TO DUST,
BUT THE TRUTHS OF THE MIND
WILL NOT BE DESTROYED.

You have no cause for anything
but *gratitude and joy.*

The mind is everything.
What you think you become.

No one saves us
but ourselves.

No one can and no one may.

We ourselves must walk the path.

There are only **two mistakes**
one can make along the road to truth;
not going all the way, and not starting.

Three things
cannot be long hidden:

the sun, the moon, and the truth.

Let your happiness depend,

not upon external things,

but upon **your own mind.**

IT IS BETTER TO
CONQUER YOURSELF
THAN TO WIN
A THOUSAND BATTLES.

It is you who must
make the effort.

Masters only point the way.

PEACE COMES
FROM WITHIN.

DO NOT SEEK
IT WITHOUT.

We are what we think.

All that we are arises with our thoughts.

With our thoughts, we make the world.

A jug fills drop by drop.

We are shaped by our thoughts;
we become what we think.

When the mind is pure, joy follows
like a shadow that never leaves.

I do not believe in a *fate*
that falls on men however they act;

but I do believe in a fate
that falls on them unless they act.

To enjoy good health, to bring true happiness to one's family, to bring peace to all, one must first discipline and control one's own mind.

If a man can control his mind he can find the way to **Enlightenment,** and all wisdom and virtue will naturally come to him.

ALL **WRONG~DOING** ARISES
BECAUSE OF MIND.

IF MIND IS TRANSFORMED CAN
WRONG~DOING REMAIN?

An insincere and evil friend
is more to be feared than a wild beast;
a wild beast may wound your body,
but an evil friend will wound your mind.

What **you are**

is what you have been.

What **you'll be**

is what you do now.

The wise ones fashioned speech

with their thought, sifting it

as grain is sifted through a sieve.

The thought manifests as the word;

the word manifests as the deed;

the deed develops into habit;

and habit hardens into character.

So watch the thought and its ways

with care, and let it spring from love

born out of concern for all beings.

Truth desires to **appear**;
truth longs to **become conscious**;
truth strives to **know itself.**

Persevere in thy quest and thou shalt
find what thou seekest.

Pursue thy aim unswervingly
and thou shalt **gain** the prize.

Struggle earnestly and thou shalt **conquer.**

He who thinks **correctly** *will rid himself of ignorance and acquire wisdom.*

The attainment of truth
is possible only when
self is recognized as an illusion.

Righteousness can be practiced
only when we have freed our mind
from the passions of egotism.

Perfect peace can dwell only
where all vanity has disappeared.

VERILY, IT IS THE DESTRUCTION, IN
WHICH NO PASSION REMAINS, OF THIS
VERY THIRST;
IT IS THE LAYING ASIDE OF,
THE BEING FREE FROM,
THE DWELLING NO LONGER
UPON THIS THIRST.

The Eightfold Path
is the way out
of suffering.

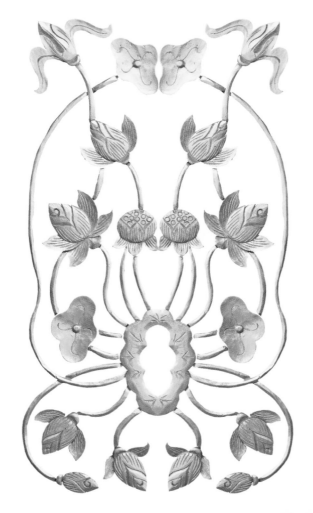

Fashion your life

as a garland of

beautiful deeds.

Always be mindful of the **kindness** and **not the faults** of others.

A noble person

is mindful and thankful for
the favors he receives from others.

He who experiences the unity of life
sees his own Self in all beings,
and all beings in his own Self,
and looks on everything
with an impartial eye.

Just as treasures are uncovered from the earth,
so **virtue** appears from good deeds,
and **wisdom** appears from
a pure and peaceful mind.

To walk safely through the maze of human life,
one needs the **light of wisdom**
and the **guidance of virtue.**

On life's journey faith is nourishment,
virtuous deeds are a shelter,
wisdom is the light by day and right
mindfulness is the protection by night.

If a man lives a pure life,
nothing can destroy him.

Teach this triple truth to all:

A generous heart, kind speech,
and a life of service and compassion
are the things which renew humanity.

To UNDERSTAND EVERYTHING
IS TO FORGIVE EVERYTHING.

The way is **not in the sky.**

The way is **in the heart.**

Endurance is one of
the most difficult disciplines,
but it is to the one who endures
that the final victory comes.

Health is the greatest gift,
contentment the greatest wealth,
faithfulness the best relationship.

DO NOT DWELL IN THE PAST,
DO NOT DREAM OF THE FUTURE,
CONCENTRATE THE MIND
ON THE **PRESENT MOMENT.**

Master your words.

Master your thoughts.

Never allow your body to do harm.

Follow these three roads with purity,
and you will find yourself upon the one way.

The way of wisdom.

Truth gives peace to the yearning mind;

it conquers error;

it quenches the flames of desires;

it leads to Nirvana.

The secret of health for both mind and body
is not to mourn for the past, worry about the future,
or anticipate troubles, but to
live in the present moment
wisely and earnestly.

It is better to

travel well

than to arrive.

When you realize how **perfect** everything is you will tilt your head back and laugh at the sky.

YOUR WORK IS TO DISCOVER YOUR
WORK AND THEN WITH ALL YOUR
HEART TO GIVE YOURSELF TO IT.

Better than a thousand
hollow words, is one word that
brings peace.

Whatever **words** we utter
should be chosen with care

for people will hear them
and be influenced by them
for good or ill.

UNTIL HE HAS UNCONDITIONAL
AND UNBIASED LOVE
FOR ALL BEINGS,
MAN WILL NOT FIND PEACE.

Thousands of candles can be lighted
from a single candle, and the life
of the candle will not be shortened.

Happiness never decreases
by being shared.

Life is so very difficult.

How can we be
anything but kind?

Charity is rich in returns; charity is the greatest wealth, for though it scatters, it brings no repentance.

IF YOU **LIGHT A LAMP**
FOR SOMEONE ELSE
IT WILL ALSO
BRIGHTEN YOUR PATH.

Let us take our refuge in the Buddha,
for he has found the everlasting in the transient.

Let us take our refuge in that which is
the immutable in the changes of existence.

Let us take our refuge in the truth
that is established through
the enlightenment of the Buddha.

Let us take our refuge in the community
of those who seek the truth
and endeavor to live in the truth.

A disciple of the Dharma will see the four noble truths and walk in the eightfold path of holiness.
He will become wary of his eye, wary of all his senses, wary of his thoughts. He will divest himself of passion and become free. He will be delivered from selfishness and attain the blessed state of Nirvana.

May all beings everywhere be happy and be free.

About Cider Mill Press Book Publishers

Good ideas ripen with time. From seed to harvest, Cider Mill Press brings fine reading, information, and entertainment together between the covers of its creatively crafted books. Our Cider Mill bears fruit twice a year, publishing a new crop of titles each spring and fall.

"Where Good Books Are Ready for Press"

Visit us on the web at
www.cidermillpress.com

or write to us at
PO Box 454
Kennebunkport, Maine 04046